ABUNDANT TRUTH INTERNATIONAL MINISTRIES

Abundant Truth Spiritual Gifts Series

THE SPIRITUAL GIFTS

A Biblical Explanation of the Gifts
of the Spirit

Roderick Levi Evans

Published by Abundant Truth Publishing
P.O. Box 126
Camden, NC 27921
Web: www.abundantpublishing.net
Email: abundantpublishing@gmail.com

Printed U.S.A.

Front & Back Cover Designs by Abundant Truth Publishing
All rights reserved.
Free-use Cover Image

> *Abundant Truth Publishing* is a ministry of **Abundant Truth International Ministries.** The primary mission of ATI Ministries is to equip the Body of Christ with tools necessary to defend and contend for the truth of the Christian faith. Jesus Christ came to bear witness of the truth and ATI Ministries is a modern-day extension of His commission (John 18:37).

Abundant Truth Spiritual Gifts Series –The Spiritual Gifts
©2021 Abundant Truth Publishing
All Rights Reserved
ISBN13: 978-1601412577

Printed in the United States of America

Unless otherwise indicated, all of the scripture quotations are taken from the *Authorized King James Version* of the Bible. Scripture quotations marked with NIV are taken from the *New International Version* of the Bible. Scripture quotations marked with NASV are taken from the *New American Standard Version* of the Bible. Scripture quotations marked with Amplified are taken from the *Amplified Bi*

Contents

Introduction

Chapter 1 – Gifts of Revelation   1

Word of Knowledge   *3*

Word of Wisdom   *9*

Discerning of Spirits   *13*

Chapter 2 – Gifts of Inspiration   23

Divers Kinds of Tongues   *25*

Interpretation of Tongues   *32*

Prophecy   *35*

Guidelines for Judging Prophecy   *41*

Chapter 3 – Gifts of Power   53

Faith   *55*

Contents *(cont.)*

Gifts of Healings — 60

Miracles — 65

Bibliography — 71

Introduction

The promise of the Father was the fulfillment of God's prophecy through Joel. One result of the Spirit's coming would be prophetic revelation and the manifestation of dreams and visions. We discover from Paul's discussions of the gifts in I Corinthian 12 that the Spirit is responsible for the dispersion of the gifts. In the Abundant Truth Spiritual Gifts Series, we will examine the gifts of the Spirit and their operations in the New Testament Church.

In this publication:

The Kingdom of God has come in power. Jesus told the disciples to go to Jerusalem and wait until they receive power (Acts 1:8). On the day of Pentecost, the disciples received the power promised to them. We will now explore Kingdom Power. God has made us partakers, not only of His nature, but also of His power.

The Kingdom of God came with ministries and gifts available to everyone under its influence. Do not be deceived; the gifts of the Holy Spirit are for today.

Though this topic has been the source of controversy for decades, believers can be confident that God is still pouring out His Spirit today. The Bible says that in the last days that he would pour out His Spirit upon all flesh.

> And it shall come to pass, saith God, I will pour forth My Spirit upon all flesh: And your sons and your daughters shall prophesy, And your young men shall see visions, And your old men shall dream dreams. Yea and on My servants and on My handmaidens in those days will I

pour forth of My Spirit; and they shall prophesy. (Acts 2:17-18 NASV)

The Old Testament scriptures also indicate that the Spirit of God would rest upon and in His people.

I will give them one heart, and I will put a new spirit within you. I will take the stony heart out of their flesh, and will give them a heart of flesh; that they may walk in my statutes, and keep mine ordinances, and do them and they shall be my people, and I will be their God. (Ezekiel 11:19-20 NASV

In this book, we will discuss the gifts and ministries of the Spirit of God, their functions, and how to recognize them in operation. God gives the Church gifts to benefit everyone. The purpose of the gifts is not to make us spiritual, but to help us to serve and minister to one another in love.

The operation of the Spirit of God and His gifts/ministries among believers testifies to the presence of God in the Church. When the gifts of the Spirit are in operation, the faith of believers is strengthened and fortified. Before examining each gift, we must realize a few facts about spiritual gifts.

> *Now there are varieties of gifts, but the same Spirit. And there are varieties of ministries, and the same Lord. And there are varieties of effects, but the same God who works all things in all persons. But to each one is given the manifestation of the Spirit for the common good. (I Corinthians 12:4-7 NASV)*

First, from the above verses, we learn that there are diversities of gifts.

God is a God of variety and He will manifest Himself in different ways. The same is true for the operation of the gifts. Second, we learn that every person has a gift.

Certain gifts are more prominent than others, but you can rest assured that God has invested a gift in you. Paul stated that God gives to "each one" a manifestation of the Spirit. Finally, we learn that not every believer possesses the same gifts. In addition, the Holy Spirit uses each person in a different manner. It is with this understanding of the gifts that we can now discuss each gift and its operation in detail.

Most commentators on the gifts and ministries of the Spirit divide them into: gifts of revelation, gifts of inspiration, gifts of power, service gifts, and ministry offices. We, too, will use these as our guides as we take a biblical approach to explain the gifts and ministries of the Spirit.

THE GIFTS OF THE SPIRIT

-Chapter 1-
Gifts of Revelation

Now concerning spiritual gifts, brethren, I would not have you ignorant. (I Corinthians 12:1 NASV)

THE GIFTS OF THE SPIRIT

THE GIFTS OF THE SPIRIT

To begin our examination of the gifts, we will look at the gifts of revelation. The gifts commonly identified as such are the word of knowledge, the word of wisdom, and the distinguishing (discerning) of spirits. They are designated as such because these gifts bring the believer into the mind of God. He becomes able to understand and see with the eyes of the Spirit.

Word of Knowledge

It is commonplace today for a believer to walk up to a brother or sister and say, "I have a word for you."

THE GIFTS OF THE SPIRIT

Oftentimes, the individual saying it has no clue what that means. As soon as we hear this expression, we think that a word of prophecy is to follow.

How many of us have been disappointed when it was something we already knew, or they only told us something that we should do? This was because they did not realize they had no word of prophecy, but only a word of knowledge or a word of wisdom.

The word of knowledge is a gift where the Spirit of God reveals facts about individuals and situations from the

THE GIFTS OF THE SPIRIT

mind of God.

I believe we all have experienced this gift in one form of another. Many times, when you know something is going to happen or when you just "know" something about an individual or situation without any outside influence; it is usually a manifestation of this gift.

When we consider the gifts of the Spirit, we feel that when God reveals something that it should be extraordinary. However, we have numerous examples in scripture where God would reveal common things to His

THE GIFTS OF THE SPIRIT

people. Therefore, when this gift manifests today outside of a ministry setting, believers overlook it occasionally.

God reveals common things through the word of knowledge. He reveals facts about certain situations. Facts revealed through the word of knowledge may deal with things in the past and present. Let us now examine the operation of this gift in scripture.

At that time Abijah the son of Jeroboam fell sick. And Jeroboam said to his wife, Arise, I pray thee, and disguise thyself, that thou be

THE GIFTS OF THE SPIRIT

not known to be the wife of Jeroboam; and get thee to Shiloh: behold, there is Ahijah the prophet, which told me that I should be king over this people. And take with thee ten loaves, and cracknels, and a cruse of honey, and go to him: he shall tell thee what shall become of the child. And Jeroboam's wife did so, and arose, and went to Shiloh and came to the house of Ahijah. But Ahijah could not see; for his eyes were set by reason of his age. And

THE GIFTS OF THE SPIRIT

the Lord said unto Ahijah, Behold, the wife of Jeroboam cometh to ask a thing of thee for her son; for he is sick: thus and thus shalt thou say unto her: for it shall be, when she cometh in, that she shall feign herself to be another woman. (I Kings 14:1-5)

Even though Ahijah was a prophet, God spoke to him through the word of knowledge. God revealed facts to him about the situation. He told him that Jeroboam's son was sick, his wife was coming, and she was pretending to be another woman.

Today, if someone has this type of information concerning a situation, we call it prophecy. Again, the word of knowledge is just what it says – knowledge concerning and surrounding certain individuals and situations.

Word of Wisdom

The word of wisdom is very similar to the w\ord of knowledge, but its function is broader. The word of wisdom gives us insight into the plan of God and shows us how to apply the word of knowledge. It does what it says; it brings

THE GIFTS OF THE SPIRIT

God's wisdom into an individual's life or situation.

It also manifests itself in the application of scripture. When we hear a minister expound upon the word of God and it comes alive to us, it is because the word of wisdom concerning that text has been given. The word of wisdom oftentimes appears in the form of a warning, telling us what we should or should not do.

The scriptures give an excellent example of this: *Now when much time was spent, and when sailing*

THE GIFTS OF THE SPIRIT

was now dangerous, because the fast was now already past, Paul admonished them, And said unto them, Sirs, I perceive that this voyage will be with hurt and much damage, not only of the lading and ship, but also of our lives. Then fearing lest we should have fallen upon rocks, they cast four anchors out of the stern, and wished for the day. And as the shipmen were about to flee out of the ship, when they had let down the boat into the sea, under colour as though they

THE GIFTS OF THE SPIRIT

would have cast anchors out of the foreship, Paul said to the centurion and to the soldiers, Except these abide in the ship, ye cannot be saved. (Acts 27:9-10, 29-31)

This is a familiar story to us all. Twice, Paul spoke up with the word of wisdom to save his life and those that were on the ship. The word of wisdom came and he told them the voyage would be deadly.

Consequently, they ignored him. After the storm arose and they were in trouble, the word of wisdom came forth again. He told them that except everyone stays on the ship, they could not be saved. They did not ignore him on this occasion; subsequently, everyone survived.

Sometimes we ignore the word of wisdom because it seems more like advice rather than revelation. We must have an ear to hear the instruction of the Spirit of God. It may mean the difference between life and death.

Discerning of Spirits

This gift has to be one of the most misunderstood gifts of those listed in I

THE GIFTS OF THE SPIRIT

Corinthians 12. To understand the true essence of this gift, we must first understand what it means to discern.

Discern means to differentiate, distinguish, observe, notice, perceive, and note. This shows us that this gift helps the believer to recognize the difference between spirits. It allows believers to know what spirit is behind any given activity.

Beloved, do not believe every spirit, but test the spirits to see whether they are from God, for many false prophets have gone out into the world. (I John 4:1 NASV)

Because the Spirit of God dwells in the each believer has the ability to discern to some degree. Yet, the individual that possesses this gift discerns with a greater level of clarity and accuracy.

They can see into the realm of the spirit and identify what spirit is in operation; whether it is the spirit of man, the Spirit of God, or the spirit of the devil.

Even during the days of the apostles, discernment was very much

THE GIFTS OF THE SPIRIT

needed. From the scriptures, we find an example of the operation of this gift.

And when Simon saw that through laying on of the apostles' hands the Holy Ghost was given, he offered them money, Saying, Give me also this power, that on whomsoever I lay hands, he may receive the Holy Ghost. But Peter said unto him, Thy money perish with thee, because thou hast thought that the gift of God may be purchased with money. Thou hast neither part nor lot in this matter:

THE GIFTS OF THE SPIRIT

for thy heart is not right in the sight of God. Repent therefore of this thy wickedness, and pray God, if perhaps the thought of thine heart may be forgiven thee. For I perceive that thou art in the gall of bitterness, and in the bond of iniquity. (Acts 8:18-23)

After addressing the foolishness of Simon's request, Peter then address the source or motivation behind his request. Peter, through the discerning of spirits, perceived that Simon had made his request because his heart was not right.

THE GIFTS OF THE SPIRIT

Peter discerned that bitterness was the poison of Simon's spirit and that iniquity had him in bondage. Peter could only make such a statement because he had discerned the spirit behind Simon's action.

Those who possess this gift must be careful not to become critical of others or become consumed with finding demonic activity. The purpose of this gift is not only for protection, but also to help us recognize God's working so that we can follow Him without fear.

THE GIFTS OF THE SPIRIT

The gifts of revelation manifest for our protection, edification, and direction. However, these gifts are ineffective if no one else knows but the recipient. Thus, the gifts of inspiration are needed to make known what is revealed through the revelatory gifts.

THE GIFTS OF THE SPIRIT

THE GIFTS OF THE SPIRIT

Notes:

_____

_____

_____

_____

_____

_____

_____

_____

_____

_____

_____

_____

THE GIFTS OF THE SPIRIT

THE GIFTS OF THE SPIRIT

-Chapter 2-
Gifts of Inspiration

THE GIFTS OF THE SPIRIT

THE GIFTS OF THE SPIRIT

As we continue our study of the gifts, we will now explore the gifts of inspiration. These are also called the vocal gifts. They are as follows: divers kinds of tongues, the interpretation of tongues, and prophecy.

Divers Kinds of Tongues

Jesus told the disciples that signs would follow anyone who believed. One of the signs was that they would speak with new tongues (Mark 16:17). The fulfillment of this prophecy happened on the day of Pentecost.

And when the day of Pentecost

THE GIFTS OF THE SPIRIT

was fully come, they were all with one accord in one place. And suddenly there came a sound from heaven as of a rushing mighty wind, and it filled all the house where they were sitting. And there appeared unto them cloven tongues like as of fire, and it sat upon each of them. And they were all filled with the Holy Ghost, and began to speak with other tongues, as the Spirit gave them utterance. (Acts 2:1-4)

Since the day of Pentecost, millions

THE GIFTS OF THE SPIRIT

have experienced this promised blessing, yet confusion remains as to its purpose and function. There are many facets to this gift.

Though we may not understand fully the use and function of this gift, we can narrow its manifestation to three things: prayer, praise, and prophecy.

Speaking and praying in tongues can prove to be a valuable part of a believer's life. Paul stated in Romans 8:26 that we do not always know what to pray for. He then says that the Spirit helps us by making intercession for us.

THE GIFTS OF THE SPIRIT

One of the ways this is done is through the gift of tongues. We should incorporate praying in the Spirit during our personal time with God (I Corinthians 14:14). Aside from making intercession for us, praying in the Spirit also edifies us. I Corinthians 14:4a NASV says,

> *One who speaks in a tongue edifies himself...*

The gift of tongues helps us to be built up in the inner man. It strengthens us. Paul, himself, understood this when he said, "I thank my God that I

THE GIFTS OF THE SPIRIT

speak with tongues more than you all (I Corinthians 14:18 NASV)."

The gift of tongues can also be used in the offering up of praise unto God. In his discussion to the Corinthian church, Paul made it clear that tongues could also be used to give adoration, blessing, and thanks unto God.

While discussing the operation of tongues, he said, "For you are giving thanks well enough (I Corinthians 14:17a NASV)." The gift of tongues can also be used to express the word of the Lord when it is followed by an interpretation.

THE GIFTS OF THE SPIRIT

Now I wish that you all spoke with tongues, but even more that you would prophesy; and greater is the one who prophesies than one who speaks in tongues, unless he interprets, so that the church may receive edifying. (I Corinthians 14:5 NASV)

Not only does the gift of tongues manifest in words that are spoken, but also in song.

What is the outcome then? I shall pray with the spirit and I shall pray with the mind also; I shall sing with the Spirit and I shall sing with the mind also (I Corinthians 14:15 NASV).

The gift of tongues can manifest in an unknown or known language. On the day of Pentecost, the tongues the disciples spoke in were unknown to them but could be understood by those listening (Acts 2:8).

Conversely, Paul states,

*For he that speaketh in an unknown tongue speaketh not unto men, but unto God; for **no man** understandeth him; howbeit in the*

Spirit he speaketh mysteries (I Corinthians 14:2 Emphasis mine)"

Interpretation of Tongues

The companion to the gift of tongues is the gift of interpretation of tongues. This gift is necessary to bring understanding to utterances that are given through the gift of tongues. We have aforementioned that the gift of tongues manifests in three ways: prayer, praise, and prophecy.

Therefore, when an utterance in tongues is given, the interpretation will fall in one of these categories. Many

THE GIFTS OF THE SPIRIT

have tried to confine the interpretation of tongues to only expressing a prophetic word.

However, the interpretation of tongues is needed to bring understanding to expressions of prayer and praise given in tongues. In this way, the whole church is edified, strengthened, and encouraged.

Wherefore let him that speaketh in an unknown tongue pray that he may interpret. For if I pray in an unknown tongue, my spirit prayeth, but my understanding is unfruitful.

THE GIFTS OF THE SPIRIT

What is it then? I will pray with the spirit, and I will pray with the understanding also: I will sing with the spirit, and I will sing with the understanding also. Else, when thou shalt bless with the spirit, how shall he that occupieth the room of the unlearned say Amen at thy giving of thanks, seeing he understandeth not what thou sayest? For thou verily givest thanks well, but the other is not edified. (I Corinthians 14:13-17)

Paul made it clear that if you speak

THE GIFTS OF THE SPIRIT

in tongues, you should ask God for the gift of interpretation. So, whether in prayer, praise, singing, it is imperative we have an understanding.

This is so the church may receive edification. The use of this gift is rarely seen in the Church today, while the gift of tongues is seen almost regularly. This was never the plan or intent of God. The challenge for us today is to seek after God that this gift would become as important as the gift of tongues.

Prophecy

"Thus saith the Lord." This is an

THE GIFTS OF THE SPIRIT

expression that some believers cannot wait to hear and an expression that some despise. In spite of these feelings, God has placed this gift in the body of Christ. It is not only reserved for those who are prophets, but for any believer whom the Spirit will use.

It is a widely publicized gift, but many are still confused about its use, function, and purpose. Whether through a prophet or layman, prophecy always comes with a purpose. In the most basic terms, prophecy comes with edification, exhortation, and comfort (console).

THE GIFTS OF THE SPIRIT

But one who prophesies speaks unto men for edification, exhortation, and consolation. One who speaks in a tongue edifies himself; but one who prophesies edifies the church. (I Corinthians 14:3-4 NASV)

Edify means to erect, build, or construct. When a word of prophecy is spoken, it should help to build up or strengthen believers in their walk with the Lord. Exhort means to encourage or provoke an action.

Many associate exhortation with

THE GIFTS OF THE SPIRIT

encouragement only. Though this is true, but there is another side to exhortation. Sometimes, exhortation is given that the people of God may repent and change their ways. The prophetic message may contain elements of rebuke through exhortation.

Comfort means to succor, help, or soothe. Oftentimes, the word of prophecy comes with a demonstration of the love and care of God for His people. This causes believers to be comforted in their trials, tests, and struggles. Whenever a word of prophecy is given, it

THE GIFTS OF THE SPIRIT

should accomplish at least one of these three.

In its simplest form to prophesy means to speak for God under divine inspiration. When someone gives a word of prophecy, it must be a "now" word; meaning, the word should be coming fresh from God.

Some things that we call prophecy are really the word of knowledge or the word of wisdom in operation. Prophecy can be predictive, but this is not its main function. Prophecy is designed to help the believer know what it is the mind and heart of God. Prophecy serves as a testimony of the Lord Jesus Christ being in the midst of His people (Revelation 19:10).

Judging prophecy can be a tough task at times. Nevertheless, the scriptures do give guidelines to us to help us as we strive to hear from God through others. We all want to receive from God, but some of us have lost faith in the gift of prophecy.

Many have received erroneous prophecies. Others have followed the directions given to them through prophecy and the results were unfavorable.

We must understand that God does speak to His people through this gift. We do not need to be afraid, but discerning. Even if we have received bad prophetic words in the past, we should not allow the enemy to steal a blessing from us. God may send someone with a valid prophetic word.

Guidelines for Judging Prophecy

When judging a prophetic word, we must be careful not to miss God. Conversely, we need to know when

THE GIFTS OF THE SPIRIT

God has not spoken. If you are unsure as to how to hear from God through others, there are certain questions you can ask yourself.

Does the prophecy come to pass? Sometimes this aspect of judging is hard to determine. However, if the person prophesying (prophet or laymen) gives a specific period or date for the word of the Lord to happen, it is easier to determine.

> *When a prophet speaketh in the name of the Lord, if the thing follow not, nor come to pass, that is the*

THE GIFTS OF THE SPIRIT

thing which the Lord hath not spoken, but the prophet hath spoken it presumptuously: thou shalt not be afraid of him. (Deuteronomy 18:22)

Conversely, do not be quick to brand the prophecy false because it did not occur when you expected it. Prayerfully consider the word. It may turn out to be valid, but you did not understand the time in which it was to happen.

Is it clear and understandable? Though God speaks to us in strange

THE GIFTS OF THE SPIRIT

ways at times, the word of the Lord should be understandable; else, you will not know what to do. You cannot obey God if the word is unclear.

For God is not the author of confusion, but of peace, as in all the churches of the saints.(I Corinthians 14:33)

On the other hand, if you do not understand the word, ask the person who delivered the word for clarity. You may find that their choice of words was not clear rather than the prophecy being bogus.

THE GIFTS OF THE SPIRIT

There may be times when the person prophesying may not know or remember what was said. However, it is our belief that if the word is from God, they should be able to explain more clearly what they received.

Does it agree with the Word? Prophecy will never instruct you to do something against the written word of God. It will agree with the Word and the Spirit in which the Word is written.

We have also a more sure word of prophecy; whereunto ye do well that ye take heed, as unto a light that shineth in a dark place, until the day of dawn, and the daystar arise in our hearts. Knowing this first that no prophecy of scripture is of any private interpretation. For the prophecy came not in old time by the will of man: but holy men of God spake as they were moved by the Holy Ghost.(2 Peter 1: 19-21)

Be humble in this area. Not every prophetic word has a direct correlation to the scripture. This is true for prophetic words that may deal with specific situations in your life. Just be sure that the word given does not tell you to do anything against the Word.

Is it demonic, fleshly, or the Spirit of God? You must learn to recognize the source of the word. Is it in agreement with the will of God for your life?

Beloved, believe not every spirit, but try the spirits whether they are of God... (I John 4:1a)

Please be wise in this area also. Sometimes, our own personal perceptions may hinder us from receiving from God. If we do not agree with a person's demeanor, we may say it

THE GIFTS OF THE SPIRIT

was flesh. Remember, God uses people. Their attributes and personality traits may surface as the Spirit moves through them. Let not your own biases block you from hearing from God.

The aforementioned guidelines are to help us in our efforts to receive from God. They are not to be used as excuses to reject the word of the Lord.

Sometimes, there will be prophetic words given to which the guidelines may tell you to reject it, but you may discover that the word is from God. Be humble and prayerful while you are trying to

THE GIFTS OF THE SPIRIT

judge the prophetic word.

Aside from revelation and inspiration, God gives us power to handle whatever revelation is given. We must now turn our attention to the gifts of power.

THE GIFTS OF THE SPIRIT

THE GIFTS OF THE SPIRIT

Notes:

THE GIFTS OF THE SPIRIT

THE GIFTS OF THE SPIRIT

-Chapter 3-
Gifts of Power

THE GIFTS OF THE SPIRIT

THE GIFTS OF THE SPIRIT

The last gifts to be explored are the gifts of power. The gifts of power demonstrate the visual manifestations of the power of God. They are as follows: gift of faith, gifts of healings, and the gift of miracles.

Faith

Every believer has been given a measure of faith (Romans 12:3). Yet, certain individuals have the gift of faith and are able to believe God for the impossible. The gift of faith may not be as "spiritual" in its manifestation as the other gifts, yet it produces results.

THE GIFTS OF THE SPIRIT

Individuals possessing this gift will be able to believe God in an unusual way and have the ability to inspire faith in others. Believers with this gift are often times viewed as radical and not in touch with reality.

Granted, we have all met people who operate in false faith. Yet, those with the gift of faith will not only believe God for the impossible but will also see the results of this kind of faith.

One of the greatest prophets that ever lived was the prophet Elijah. He is a man that demonstrated faith. However,

THE GIFTS OF THE SPIRIT

we understand that his faith was a gift from God. For when Jezebel threatened Elijah, he fled in fear (I Kings 19:1-3). Let us look at the gift of faith in Elijah in operation.

> *And Elijah the Tishbite, who was of the inhabitants of Gilead, said unto Ahab, As the Lord God liveth before whom I stand, there shall not be dew nor rain these years, but according to my word. The word of the Lord came unto him saying... (I Kings 17:1-2a)*

Even though he was a prophet,

THE GIFTS OF THE SPIRIT

Elijah did not prophesy at this time. He did not say, "Thus saith the Lord," nor "the word of the Lord came unto me saying," nor "God commanded me to say." He only spoke in faith.

Moreover, because of the gift of faith in him, he believed that God would back what he stated. The word of the Lord came to him afterwards. From further study, we find that it did not rain for over three years (James 5:17).

Christians with this gift have the ability to move in this level of faith. The

THE GIFTS OF THE SPIRIT

gift of faith operates frequently with the other gifts of the Spirit, especially healing and miracles.

Ministers commonly have this gift in their ministries, but all believers are candidates for it. We have all met believers who have extraordinary testimonies of how they believed God for the impossible.

Listening to their testimonials can make us feel that our faith is inadequate. Oftentimes, the believer telling the story has the gift of faith and may not recognize it.

THE GIFTS OF THE SPIRIT

Gifts of Healings

Along with the gifts of revelation and knowledge, God has also left gifts of healing to the Church. God also provides relief and freedom from physical ailments through the gifts of healing. It is interesting to note here that the scriptures read "gifts" of healing and not "gift." It is plural.

It is our belief then that there are different manifestations of the gifts of healing. This means that individuals with the gifts of healing may have the ability to heal certain ailments consistently.

THE GIFTS OF THE SPIRIT

For instance, one believer may have the ability to heal blind, deaf, dumb, and lame individuals, while others are gifted to heal those with cancers, diseases, and other maladies of the body consistently.

We have numerous examples in scripture that demonstrate the gifts of healing in operation. Healing can be administered in various ways. Healing can take place through the spoken word, through the laying on of hands, and other means.

Oftentimes, healing will take place after the manifestation of the word or

THE GIFTS OF THE SPIRIT

knowledge. God will reveal the ailment and then heal. Other times, healing will take place during prayers of confession and repentance. Healings may take place after prophetic utterances have occurred as a sign of God's presence and favor.

How the gifts of healing are manifest will vary from believer to believer. Yet, those with gifts of healing will accomplish the same goal: provide healing.

Now Peter and John went up together into the temple at the

THE GIFTS OF THE SPIRIT

hour of prayer, being the ninth hour. And a certain man lame from his mother's womb was carried, whom they laid daily at the gate of the temple which is called Beautiful, to ask alms of them that entered into the temple; Who seeing Peter and John about to go into the temple asked an alms. And Peter, fastening his eyes upon him with John, said, Look on us. And he gave heed unto them, expecting to receive something of them. Then Peter said, Silver and gold have I

THE GIFTS OF THE SPIRIT

none; but such as I have give I thee: In the name of Jesus Christ of Nazareth rise up and walk. (Acts 3:1-6)

From this passage, we find that healing was administered through the spoken word. Peter said to the man that what he had he would give him.

What did he have? Healing. And after speaking the word of healing, he helped him up and God confirmed the word. We can rejoice and be glad that gifts of healing are still in operation today.

THE GIFTS OF THE SPIRIT

Miracles

A miracle is a supernatural act or event. As with the other gifts, miracles are available to believers. Miracles are not the same as healing, as some think. Miracles are "acts" or events that are strange and abnormal. Though healings may be strange and unusual, they occur through the gifts of healing.

Examples of miracles range from making an axe head float to men walking on water. Paul the apostle had miracles in his ministry.

And God wrought special miracles

THE GIFTS OF THE SPIRIT

by the hands of Paul. (Acts 19: 11)

We know that cloths and aprons do not have power to heal and cast out devils. Through the gift of miracles, aprons and cloths taken from Paul's body healed the sick and cast out devils. The gift of miracles is an unusual gift that brings the supernatural acts of God to men.

Remember, no matter what gifts God has given you; use them in the Spirit of love. Having gifts without love does not mean anything (I Corinthians 13).

THE GIFTS OF THE SPIRIT

However, every gift must be used in faith.

If you feel God has given you gifts, do not be afraid to exercise them. God may want you to be a blessing. If you are unsure, pray and seek God. Then, talk to your leader about it and other mature saints. God gives gifts to be used and not buried.

THE GIFTS OF THE SPIRIT

THE GIFTS OF THE SPIRIT

Notes:

_____

_____

_____

_____

_____

_____

_____

_____

_____

_____

_____

_____

THE GIFTS OF THE SPIRIT

Bibliography

Evans, Roderick L. Kingdom Practice, Power, and Principle Writers Club Press. Lincoln, NE, c2002

Lockman Foundation. Comparative Study Bible. Zondervan Publishing House. Grand Rapids, MI, c1984

Tucker, Ron & Hufton, Rick. God's Plan For Christian Service. Grace Church. St. Louis, MO, c1987

THE GIFTS OF THE SPIRIT

The Bible Library. The Bible Library CD Rom Disc. Ellis Enterprises Incorporated, (c) 1988 – 2000. 4205 McAuley Blvd., Suite 385, Oklahoma City, OK 73120. All Rights Reserved.

THE GIFTS OF THE SPIRIT

Notes:

THE GIFTS OF THE SPIRIT